What the wrong kind of love taught me

A Singles Journey to Wholeness

Written By:
Celena Powell

Scripture quotations are taken from the *Holy Bible*, New Living
Translation, copyright ©1996, 2004, 2007 by Tyndale House
Foundation; the *Holy Bible,* King James Version. New York:
American Bible Society: 1999 Holy Bible, King James Version,
copyright © 1999 by New York: Bible Society; and the *Holy Bible,*
Amplified Version, *Copyright © 2015.*

Printed in the United States of America

THIS BOOK IS NOT INTENDED TO BE A HISTORY TEXT.
While every effort has been made to check the accuracy of dates,
locations, and historical information, no claims are made as to the
accuracy of such information.

INFORMATION IN THIS BOOK DOES NOT REPRESENT THE
VIEWS OF DUDLEY PUBLISHING HOUSE OR ANY OF IT'S
SUBSIDIARIES.
For book orders, author appearance inquires and interviews, contact
the author:

ISBN-978-1-7365810-3-2

Dudley Publishing House

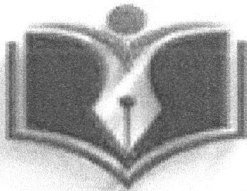

Dudley Publishing
HOUSE

www.dudleypublishinghouse.net

Dedication

This Book is dedicated to all those who taught me what love is by showing me what love is not!

Thank you. Without your lessons, I would have never learned how to love.

Acknowledgments

I give thanks to Jehovah, the Great I AM. God Thank you for being patient with me and for not letting go of my hand even when I withdrew my hand from you. YOU ARE MY EVERYTHING!

To my mother H. Marie Daniels, thank you for your being my SHERO! Your love, strength, and prayers have sustained me.

To my sons Andrew and Mark, thank you for allowing me to mother you, you are my heartbeats, your lives are God's reminder of how much He loves me.

To My Great Aunt and Uncle the late Mr. and Mrs. William E. Walker, thank you for showing me at an early age what unconditional love looks and feels like. I miss you both every day, thank you for being my Guardian Angles, Rest in The Masters' Arms until we meet again.

To all of my Spiritual Midwives and Sisters too numerous to mention, please know all that I am is because you love me enough to tell me the truth, I love you all!

Content

Preface
The Struggle

THE STRUGGLE IS REAL! Having been married and divorced not once but three times, I could have never imagined that being Saved and Single would be the most challenging journey I'd take in life. Having been raised in the Church, having a father who's a Pastor, having attained a degree from a Bible college, serving in ministry at various capacities, I still found myself void of the one thing I longed for, the love of a man who would love me the way I desired to be loved. Yes, I know God loves me, yes, I know Jesus loves me too, but I still longed for what I thought I was missing, only to find it wasn't lost, I just lacked the wisdom and understanding of what Love truly is and what it is not.

The singles in the church have been taught to say "I'm single, saved and satisfied." or you may hear "God/Jesus is my husband, I'm good..." Singles in the Church are made to feel as if you can't be "sanctified" and sexy and still saved and filled with the Holy Spirit. So often we suffer in what I call "silent sin", not because we're wicked, but we feel as if we have no one to be transparent with. We oftentimes feel abandoned or thought of as an afterthought by the "Church Folks", the truth of the matter is the Church is challenged with how to deal with such a vast group of people.

As you read through this study, I pray that my journey to Wholeness while walking in Singleness, can be used as a tool and testament that being single is not void of being whole, nor are you alone.

God's word, being honest and patient with myself, and embracing my singleness has set me free.

Ready? Let's journey.

Introduction

The Desire

I Corinthians 13:4-8 NIV

"Love is patient, love is kind. It does not envy, it does not boast, it is not proud. It does not dishonor others, it is not self-seeking, it is not easily angered, it keeps no record of wrongs. Love does not delight in evil but rejoices with the truth. It always protects, always trusts, always hopes, always perseveres. Love never fails…"

The desire to be loved and give love is our indication that we are alive; the feeling of being in love and giving love provides a sense of security. The need for us to be needed and accepted speaks to our self-worth, we place an enormous amount of value on what we feel should and could be opposed to what we know to be true. The world we live in has tainted the true meaning of love, love is not just an emotion, it's a choice! In order to love, we must first properly define love. For me, Jesus is the ultimate example of pure love. Love is sacrificial, it is committed, it is focused, and doesn't waver.

You can't love someone unless you learn to love yourself first. You must understand that love will mean sacrifice, commitment, it is a choice, not just an emotion. Loving yourself will require a great deal of inside-out work.

Deliverance from past hurts, disappointments, let downs, broken relationships, failures, childhood hurt, loss of loved ones, emotional wounds, all play in how we give and receive love.

My first introduction to love beyond that of my parents was around the age of 5. I recall attending church with my grandmother and mother. Going to church and Sunday school every Sunday. We had children's church after Sunday School, and this is where God's Love for me became personal. I recited it over and over, learning it by heart. We have taught 1 Corinthians 13 the famous "love" scripture. I have recited this scripture 100's of times, and yet I have found myself in relationships that were destructive, unedifying, unloving, disrespectful, soul sabotaging, and if I had remained could have led to my death in the natural and spiritual. I would find myself in the same kind of relationship repeatedly, and I'd end up feeling empty, lost, and lonely. One day I realized that the "holes in my soul" were the root of my relational retardation; I needed to take a deep look within, get down and dirty with me, I had to deal with some harsh truths about my decisions and choices when it came to dating and marriage and ask God to deliver me from me!

The First Step in the process of deliverance is being honest with self, admitting to the "hurting you" that you need to be healed from the inside out. Now to be clear, deliverance can be instantaneous, however, healing is a process! There is no quick-fix when it comes to matters of the heart- prayer, fasting and time are God's tools He has provided to assist in the repairing of our souls. No one can fill the emptiness in you, only Jesus can do that, but you must first understand that being a Whole person begins with you, not relying on someone else to "fix" you or to come alongside you and "make you whole"; two half-persons do not make a whole person, hurting people hurt people and the cycle of hurt only ends when we decide to resolve our internal unresolved issues.

Now I will tell you, my journey has been painful, lonely, hard and at times confusing, but God! I have fallen so many times, been in a backslid position, turned away from God's way, and this is since I've been saved! So please understand, the journey you are about to embark on as you turn these pages, I too, continue to posture myself in a place of humility asking God for strength, giving me His ability to keep me strong when I am weak.

At the end of lessons 1-4, we will *unpack some of the root causes that have led to poor decision making in relationships.* The more we unpack the more room we make for God to lead and guide our decision making before entertaining dating.

In lessons 5 and 6 we will begin to r e - *pack* our love suitcases with God's truths about self, self-love, and loving others. This is going to change the way we view ourselves from the inside-out.

NOW LET'S JOURNEY!

1

Internal Bleeding

Luke 8:43-44 MSG

"In the crowd that day there was a woman who for twelve years had been afflicted with hemorrhages. She had spent every penny she had on doctors but not one had been able to help her..."

I love the account of the woman with the issue of blood, she is unnamed in the Gospel of Luke, however, her testimony has been preached to millions of people over two thousand years later. I believe she was a single woman for three reasons, 1. She was considered to be unclean therefore a man during these times would not have taken her to be his wife. 2. The account tells us that she had spent all she had looking to be cured, with no mention of a husband providing support. 3. There is no mention of a husband in the story.

The story tells us that she struggled with an issue for twelve years, with no cure in sight! I imagine her feeling empty, unworthy, ugly, lonely, not good enough, unworthy, helpless, hopeless, depressed, and desperate. I identify with her in so many ways, I believe all that are reading this see yourselves or have seen yourselves in one or more of these ways while walking in singleness.

LET'S DEAL WITH IT!

Having dated, been married and now single (single for many years), I know what it's like to dress up my outer appearance while neglecting my inner self. I know all too well how to dress-up, mask my face with make-up, dress my body in an outfit, and wear shoes that will "preach"! I'm doing all this having a pretty decent career, making decent money, being educated, and serving in ministry, yet still, I am ill on the inside with no healing in sight.

What was my illness you ask; the Spirit of loneliness and lust was oozing from my Spirit controlling my flesh! See it didn't matter that I had been saved for over 30 years, or that my daddy is a Pastor or my momma was praying for me daily, nor did my serving in the church ministry having a title or praying on a regular for others and myself… the bleeding wouldn't stop.

I couldn't talk to church folks, tried that, all I got was "pray, fast and pray, just be patient..." or "God got you…it's all in God's timing…" Now let me just say, this is all good, sounds good, is the correct council, and can and does work. However, having been married I know what companionship looks and feels like. I know what it's like to have desires that God approves of in the sanctity of marriage, so it's a lot more challenging to go from having to being without.

When looking at the woman with the issue of blood, I purposely used the part of the scripture that speaks to her issue before healing takes place for lesson one. If truth be told, your issue isn't external, it's internal, you have the external perfected, but you're hemorrhaging internally and have tried everything to mask the spirit of loneliness or lust or both.

You are not alone! There's absolutely nothing to be ashamed of, God created us for companionship, we've just hit a bump in the road. God is using your journey in singleness to find your wholeness! I submit to you that the woman with the issue of blood is like so many of us who walk in singleness, we will date men we know matter-of-factly are no good, we will settle for a 'piece' of a man out of fear of being lonely, we feel unworthy at times in a world that has placed great emphasis on being "booed-up", we feel unworthy when a man that we have poured into rejects us, and there are times where we feel hopelessly wandering because it appears everyone has someone and we're still single.

Now let's pause, we have some unpacking to do before we continue...

LET'S UNPACK HERE!

In this section, we will *unpack* some things that have caused *internal bleeding* in your Spirit. Remember, the key to your journey to wholeness begins with inside out work, so you must be honest with yourself to get delivered from you!

Now let's begin to *unpack* by answering the questions below.

1. How/Why are you single? (e.g Divorced/Never been married)

2. What has been the greatest struggle in your singleness?

3. Why do you believe you struggle in that

    area mentioned in question #2?

4. What has your struggle cost you?

Love Taught Me | Celena Powell

I know the *unpacking* is uncomfortable, but I want you to envision the woman with the issue of blood. Think about how uncomfortable she must have felt. She literally placed her life in danger by being out among the crowd in her condition. The law of the land considered her to be "unclean" and contaminated, yet she risked her life and exposed her illness to be healed!

In this season of singleness, use your time of oneness to find your wholeness! Dig deep, be willing to fight through a crowd of struggles that you just unpacked! Press your way through to get delivered and healed from past hurt, past disappointments, failed relationships, slip-ups, wrong choices, and bad decisions. The more we unpack, the more we look inward, the closer we get to our deliverance that opens the door to wholeness.

Now let's journey On.

2

The Spirit of Loneliness

II Tim. 1:7 AMP

"For God did not give us a spirit of timidity or cowardice or fear, but [He has given us a spirit] of power and of love and of sound judgment and personal discipline [abilities that result in a calm, well-balanced mind and self-control]."

The spirit of loneliness is very real, however,

when we take a deeper look, this is F.E.A.R.

(False Evidence Appearing Real). Oftentimes we

spend a considerable amount of time rehearsing the, "what if's, what may happen, why it hasn't happened" or we live in self-condemnation of our history of unsuccessful relationships. Replaying these thoughts leads to anxiety, thus making us believe we are lonely or will be lonely for the rest of our lives.

Miriam Webster Dictionary defines fear as 1). to be afraid of *(something or someone)* 2). to expect or worry about *(something bad or unpleasant)* or 3). to be afraid and worried. This definition substantiates my belief that fear is the root cause of most singles' emotional distress and once identified can be a major breakthrough on the road to Wholeness!

In Lesson 1 we glanced at the story of the woman with the issue of blood, we noted that she dealt with loneliness due to her physical condition. But if we take a closer look, we can imagine that her issues were not only external, they were internal as well. Although she was healed, I would submit to you that she still had to deal with thoughts that took root while dealing with her issue; she is now challenged to live a life of normalcy. This means she has to deal with the internal mental scars that haunt her, probably wondering "what if people don't believe she's healed, she's probably assuming she may still be ostracized, or maybe no one will ever love her.

Fear can cause you to make what's not reality

seem real! When I tell you, I lived like this for *years*! I was dealing with the internal voids, the voices in my head, making my past disappointments my present truth, I gave fiction an open door to destroy my future.

As I began to process why I kept attracting and dealing with the same kind of men, the same familiar spirits, I knew deep within me I needed to take a look inward and do some much-needed gutting out! Even as I type these words, my heart cries for those, who like me, desire wholeness in mind, body, and spirit, but find themselves in a cycle of dysfunctional choices when it comes to love.

We must decide what we believe and begin to navigate accordingly. We have to deal with the questions in lesson 1, what our greatest struggles are in singleness and why this particular area has been so challenging. For me, it was the Spirit of Loneliness, which I have determined to be rooted in fear. I sincerely believe, most singles are truly dealing with fear and don't even realize this is one of the root causes of their relational dysfunction.

The Creator God has told us He "has not given us a spirit of timidity or cowardice or fear, but [He has given us a spirit] of power and love and of sound judgment and personal discipline [abilities that result in a calm, well- balanced mind and self-control]." It's time to look inward, dig deep, and again *unpack*. Listen, the purge is necessary, your wholeness is worth you dismissing everything that has kept you in bondage and broken.

Now let's pause, we have more unpacking to do before we continue...

LET'S UNPACK HERE!

In this section, we will *unpack* The *Spirit of Loneliness*. Remember, the key to your journey to wholeness begins with inside out work, so you must be honest with yourself to get delivered from you!

Now let's begin to *unpack* by answering the questions below.

1. Has loneliness been an issue for you?

2. How has loneliness affected your dating?

3. Do you fear you'll never find that special someone?

4. What changes in your thinking can you apply immediately to combat your fear?

You're on your way to wholeness, making significant progress! As you continue to *unpack* all the excess baggage you will have room to replace your spirit with what's required to be whole! This is hard work and painful but getting to the root of an issue requires you to dig deep!

Finding you, in the season of singleness is imperative. So many people think the answer to happiness is finding their significant other when the truth is happiness begins and ends from within! You must be a whole complete person in order to love and receive love.

Now let's journey on.

3

The Empty Well

John 4:15-17 NIV

"The woman said to him, Sir, give me this water so that I won't get thirsty and have to keep coming here to draw water. He told her, Go, call your husband, and come back. I have no husband, she replied."

I remember feeling so broken emotionally when my oldest sons' father and I separated and ultimately divorced. My fairytale of love and marriage fell apart and I felt cheated, helpless, ashamed, scared, and alone. This was not the way

I planned my life, I was the girl who was supposed to have the husband, the house, and the kids and lives happily-ever-after, so how could this be.

WHEN I met my youngest sons' father, I was so wounded, we met, briefly dated, I got pregnant, had our son, and were married shortly thereafter. I wanted desperately to be loved, I still longed to have my fairy- tale family, the husband, the kids, and a home that was filled with love. Seven years later, I found myself divorced yet again, still lonely, and longing for someone to love me the way that I love and yet I was still empty inside.

Just as another marriage was ending, I caught

the interest of a co-worker, who would end up being my 3rd husband in less than a year of me divorcing my second husband. This man got me by way of familiarity. He happened to be from my hometown, found out he knew and went to school with my cousins, and his sisters went to school with my brother. I had no idea that this would end up being my lowest point in life, I would find myself over the next five years in survival mode.

This part of my journey is extremely difficult for me to write, as I buried this marriage in several pieces in the cemetery of my memory, in unmarked graves to never revisit. I was so desperate to be loved, that I purposely ignored all of the red flags, and trust me, they were blazing red, and I refused to acknowledge them. This relationship was tumultuous, to say the least. I endured multiple beatings, I was degraded verbally and emotionally, taunted, manipulated, lied to, and lied on, isolated, and my children were innocent witnesses.

Like the woman at the well when she told Jesus "...Sir you have nothing to draw with and the well is deep...", I felt as if I had nothing to "draw" a loving, caring God-fearing, decent man with. I had already given up; I didn't believe that God cared about me being happy in finding love. I was so broken, and empty inside, I would constantly replay the statement that husband #3 would say to me, "...nobody is going to want you with two kids..., and knowing you been married three times..."

After multiple calls to the police for domestic violence, my ex-husband being incarcerated on more than one occasion for domestic violence, you'd think I would have left him, but I had no strength or any amount of self-love to do so. It wasn't until the abuse threatened my children that I decided to divorce him.

The feeling of embarrassment, unworthiness, unlovable, and being a disappointment to all of the people who held me in high regard, even the feeling of God punishing me for making such a bad decision caused me to turn so inward and see love in a very distorted way.

As the years went by, I dated and found myself in relationships with personality types that were contrary to what I knew in my heart I wanted. Men making the same empty promises, having the same characteristics as the last guy, nothing really lasting, nor fulfilling. The desire to be married was my focus, but I didn't understand that I needed to be delivered and healed from all my brokenness.

At one point, I decided to give up on love, the possibility of finding someone that wanted to love me, seemed unlikely. I started to feel as if I was unlovable, this left me empty and somewhat bitter.

Then the year 2015 came, I thought this was a turning point, I had been divorced for quite some time, I was about to be an empty nester, my oldest was graduating high school going off to college, and my youngest living with his dad, I was open to new possibilities, I had been dating a guy for about a year, long-distance who lived in Ohio. By now, I thought I was on the right track, I had prayed and specifically told God that I did not want to date anyone I had to get-to-know, I specifically prayed that the man I'd meet and eventually marry would be from my home town, and I'd already know him and along came that guy, he wasn't from my hometown, but we attended the same college in Ohio so of course, I just knew he was the *one*!

That same year I was recruited by a

company in Ohio, which was about three hours from my hometown. After a lengthy interview process, I was offered the position, and off I went! I moved to a new city, where I didn't know a soul, I was living about three hours from my hometown where I grew up, and the guy I was dating lived about an hour-and-a-half away so finally the love I wanted was within my reach, so I thought, only to be disappointed yet again. Here I was isolated and lonely; how could this be?

Then, an acquaintance from my past came along, but hold-up, he was from my hometown!!! Yes, this has got to be it, I knew him, he was successful in his career, he was easy on the eyes, charming, respectful, intelligent, and funny, and appeared to be loving and caring. Now initially I wasn't interested in dating him, as a matter-of-fact, early into the relationship I told him several times I didn't think it was a good idea for him and I to date! I told him this on at least 4 separate occasions, and each time he assured me that I'd be making a huge mistake, he assured me he was the man for me and I was the woman for him.

Right here is where I realized my thirst was real! I knew this man was not willing to love me the way I needed to be loved, I allowed him to give me bits and pieces of

him at his leisure while I gave him all of
me, I was holding on to promises of us
getting married, I believe him when he told
me he loved me, even when his actions
were contrary to what he was saying. I was
in Love, with the promises he made, not the
reality of what the relationship was. Like all
the other relationships, he too walked away,
and I was left alone at my Well asking God
to fill me!

My thirst to be loved created a soul tie that cost me almost three years to get delivered from. I was like the woman at the well that came to draw water in the dark. She wanted to be loved, no matter what the cost. She risked her reputation, she laid aside her morals, her thirst to be loved misguided her to the point where having had five husbands taught her nothing. She is on man number six, who in her mind, I'm sure has already taken her to the altar and said "I do", and yet she still thirst because she's empty! I can so relate to the woman Jesus met at the well, yearning to be loved, still seeking for my definition of love in all the wrong places.

When we are not whole, the holes in our Spirit we'll attract *dry spirits*, these types of spirits will create dry places that will draw more dry Spirits which create deficits in our emotions. The cycle of one relationship after another is indicative of our *spiritual Well* being empty. What we are void of will begin to dictate our decisions, which lead to cycles of bad choices, thus leaving us as singles in a constant state of thirst!

The woman at the Well thirst is representative of the flesh wanting what the flesh wants, negating the spirit. When our spirit is at dis-ease our flesh is open to worldly lust; the more we feed the flesh, the weaker our Spirit becomes. Being single has its challenges no doubt! But going from one relationship to the next can lead to a desolate place and utter brokenness, however, do not be dismayed, once identified and honestly dealt with, your Spiritual Well can be refilled and never run dry!

Now let's pause, we have some unpacking to do before we continue.

LET'S UNPACK HERE!

In this section, we will *unpack The Empty Well*. Remember, the key to your journey to wholeness begins with inside out work, so you must be honest with yourself to get delivered from YOU!

Now let's begin to *unpack* by answering the questions below.

1. How do you identify with the Woman at the Well as it relates to dating?

2. What is attracting/has attracted you to this man?

3. What are you/have you been
   THIRSTY for in a relationship?

4. Name one change can you apply
   immediately to combat your Thirst?

Now I know looking inward can be rough, but please know your journey to wholeness is dependent upon the work you put in! God is committed to us being a complete person in Spirit, Mind, and Body, however, he requires us to put in the work!

As I write this, know that I am still on the journey with you! Although I have overcome many obstacles in my Singleness, I ask God every day to give me strength and to keep me as only he can. When I feel myself getting weak, I allow myself to cry, talk to God, get angry, and recall all that God has promised me.

God promised us that He will never leave us nor forsake us! Don't be afraid to open your mouth and speak aloud what God has promised you!

Now let's journey on.

4

Rejection

Gen. 29:31-32 NIV

"When the Lord saw that Leah was not loved, he enabled her to conceive, but Rachel remained childless. Leah became pregnant and gave birth to a son. She named him Reuben, for she said, "It is because the Lord has seen my misery. Surely my husband will love me now."

In the book of Genesis on the 29th, we meet Leah, a woman who is desperate for love. She finds herself in a situation where no matter what she does to win the love of her husband nothing works. She gives birth to four sons, and each time believes the man she loves will give her his heart and to no avail, it never happens.

How many times have you found yourself in Leah's shoes? How many times have you given your body or your time to a man who didn't love you the way you loved him? Or maybe you've used your skills by helping him advance in his career, or you could be supporting him financially, or it could be a combination of all the above. I am sure as a single, you have found yourself going above and beyond giving boyfriends "Husband" benefits.

How we see and feel about ourselves often

determines what we tolerate and how we engage in relationships. Can I be transparent? I, like Leah, believed the more I gave to a man, rather it is physical, monetary, or my time, he'd love me because he'd find value in that. In the end, nothing I did was ever enough, and they would eventually leave and there I was once again, patching pieces of my broken heart back together. I would convince myself that there was something wrong with "him", not realizing that the common denominator was me!

I can remember crying and begging men to stay in my life. I couldn't wrap my mind around why they would want to leave me. I couldn't understand why I wasn't enough. I thought if I was pretty enough, educated enough, lovable enough, I just wasn't enough. Like Leah I kept thinking, okay, I did this or that and now, he will surely love me.

From what we know of Leah, she was considered to be unattractive, it is said that her name meant "weary" or by some translation's "cow". Understanding culturally, names that were given to people during this time were representative of how the parents viewed their children's future, their names were prophetic. I imagine Leah had very low self-esteem, she probably believed she wasn't worthy of Love, she probably assumed she'd never marry or have children. I think it may be safe to assume that Leah may have felt rejection from her parents, being that they named her according to how they viewed her.

Our parents are our first teachers of everything, especially love. Their acceptance of us is our guidebook of how we view ourselves; it is how we learn "Love", our parents' approval is what we set out to gain and we will measure every relationship we enter using this compass. For me my parents' approval was everything, I never wanted to disappoint them. Not to mention I had the "church folks" glaring at me, I was even told by a Pastor, "you don't have time to grieve/cry; you got to suck that up…move on.."

Looking back on my childhood and teen years, I realize my parents' divorce played a huge role in how I viewed relationships. It shaped how I sought the love of a man. I was 12 when my parents' divorce. My father was absent for many years before the divorce. I was his Princess, he always protected me, and I always felt safe. My dad was my protector, he spoiled me, then abruptly he was gone! The 12-year-old girl trapped in the 40-something-year-old body was and has been seeking the love of her father that was lost. This optical way of thinking has caused me to look for the wrong kind of love in relationships.

My Fathers absences told the 12-year-old girl she was "rejected", she was no longer lovable or worthy of love or the attention and the protection all young girls need from their father. In writing this journal, I was able to identify the root of my fear of rejection, this in itself is therapeutic for me. It helped me face my demon of rejection. I had to literally tell the 12-year-old Celena, "Baby, you were not rejected, you were loved and still loved by your father, his distancing himself from you was not about you, it was about him, he was fighting his own demons, you just happen to be in the line of fire".

When I tell you, getting to the root of my

issues with rejection is delivering me as I type these words! I had to forgive my father, and then release the 12year old little girl to forgive the 49-year-old woman, remember your singleness is a journey, and deliverance is a process.

Like Leah, God is opening our wounded wombs, He is delivering us, healing one

wound at a time by opening our eyes of understanding. He hears our cries for help, even if we don't ask for it.

Now let's pause, we have some unpacking to do before we continue...

LET'S UNPACK HERE!

IN THIS section we will **UNPACK** the *Rejection*. Remember, the key to your journey to wholeness begins with inside out work, so you must be honest with yourself to get delivered from YOU!

Now let's begin to UNPACK by answering the questions below.

1. How do you identify with Leah as it relates to rejection?

2. What is the root of your issues with rejection?

3. How has the fear of rejection affected your decisions in dating?

4. Name one change/do can you apply immediately to combat your fear of Rejection.

5

The Reckoning

(John.5:6&8 NIV)

When Jesus saw him lying there and learned that he had been in this condition for a long time, he asked him, "Do you want to get well?.. Then Jesus said to him, "Get up! Pick up your mat and walk." At once the man was cured; he picked up his mat and walked.

Now that we have identified internal and external factors that have caused us to make the choices we've made in relationships, it's time to get up and move forward. To do so, we must begin to replace our "spiritual suitcases" with healthy weight! You did not enter this journey with me to just read, little did you know this is your appointed hour to take up your mat and WALK!

Like the man that was laying at the pool of Bethesda, who had been sick, paralyzed for 38 years; laying in his pity, blaming others for his inability to get his healing, when all the while the power lies within him to be healed! I believe you have it in you to begin your healing process! Now Pick up your Mat and WALK!

When we realize that we are a "WHOLE" person in our singleness, and how important it is to know that we have the power within us to lead happy whole lives we will no longer accept anything less than God's best for us.

Know let me preference this by saying, your journey to WHOLENESS is just that a journey! Do not be dismayed when you find yourself visiting dark places in your past, this is going to happen from time-to-time, just remember you CAN'T stay there! It's imperative to allow yourself to cry, mourn, be angry, scream, shout, and vent if necessary, but again, remember you CAN'T stay in that space, you have to PICK UP YOUR MAT and walk!

Now let's pause, we have some

PACKING to do before we continue...

LET'S PACK HERE!

In this section, we will begin to **PACK**. Remember, the key to your journey to wholeness begins with inside out work, so you must be honest with yourself to prepare for the **NEW YOU**!

Now let's begin to PACK by answering the questions below.

1. Name three things you need to forgive yourself for and forgive yourself right NOW!

2. Name 3 people in past relationships you need to forgive. Forgive them Right NOW!

3. you have accomplished in your life, no matter how small you think they are. Meditate on these accomplishments and CELEBRATE YOU!

4. Name 3 Strengths that you have in

any area of your life, meditate this week on these traits.

5. Dedicate one hour a day to quieting your mind and spirit. Spend time in prayer, worship, and meditation. (This should be incorporated into your daily routine).

6. Name 3 things you've learned about yourself this week.

6

The Reckoning

(Isaiah 43:18&19 NIV)

"Remember ye, not the former things, neither consider the things of old. Behold, I will do a new thing; now it shall spring forth; shall ye not know it? I will even make a way in the wilderness, and rivers in the desert."

God is the Master of making all things in our lives NEW! I know letting go of the old you can be difficult; sometimes we become accustom to functioning in our dysfunction!

It's easy for our unhealthy behavior to become the norm in our lives. But once you identify actions that are contrary to what keeps you free in mind body and spirit, change is required.

In Lessons 1-4, you have identified internal and external factors that have held you hostage and bound; making several bad choices, living with regrets, feeling isolated, maybe even trapped- but know God has a plan, and that plan requires you to forget the "old you", and begin to embrace the New You!

Just when you may have thought all was lost, or your life as a single could not be fulfilling, or you had given up on finding love, GOD is saying to you right NOW HE IS DOING A NEW THING in and with you. All the places in your life that were dry, barren, void, dark, disappointing are being rejuvenated. You are putting in the work that is essential to your WHOLENESS!

Remember your being and maintaining WHOLENESS is a Journey! Just like a car, regular maintenance is mandatory internally as well as external for you to function properly. The shedding of the old you makes way for the new you! Like you, I too continue a journey to make room for the new me.

This journey is assisting you with your makeover by uprooting all of the lies, shame, guilt, misinformation, and condemnation you may have been living with for years. The work you put into yourself is worth the investment, there's nothing better than yielding a return on a sure thing! YOU ARE WORTH IT!

Time is or greatest commodity, although you may feel as if you've wasted time, or there's no hope for you, know this, GOD can redeem the TIME! God is not subject to our time-keeping, he can do in a month what may take you and me to do in our own strength a year to accomplish. Don't waste another moment in the past, take your authority and live in your right now, it's a new you emerging, be ready to meet the NEW YOU!

As we get ready to close out this journey, we still have some packing to do…

Now let's pause, we have some *PACKING* to do before we continue...

LET'S PACK HERE!

In this section, we will begin to **PACK**. Remember, the key to your journey to wholeness begins with inside out work, so you must be honest with yourself to prepare for the **NEW YOU!**

1. Name three things new things you've learned about yourself in this journey!

2. Name 3 changes you are going to make immediately

3. What has the wrong kind of love taught you?

4. Choose 1 of the 3 people you need to forgive and write them a letter. (you can mail it to them or keep it as a reminder that you've forgiven them)

5. Purchase a journal and write in it daily or at minimum weekly (this will help you track and maintain your thoughts).

6. Name 3 things you've learned about yourself this week.

7. Meditate on Isiah 43:18-19, I suggest printing out the scripture and placing it somewhere life the refrigerator or bathroom mirror.

8. Write yourself a love letter! Begin to love on yourself, if you can't love yourself, it's impossible to love someone else.

Although we have come to the end of this part of our journey, know that this is just the beginning of what GOD is doing in your Singleness. Learn to embrace this process, there is so much to learn about you. There is so much to see, observe, and prepare for.

It is my sincere prayer that my sharing my journey and some of the tools I have used and am still using will Minister to your Spirit and set you FREE!

MY NAME IS CELENA, I AM HERE TO BREAK YOU OUT OF THE STRUGGLE OF SINGLENESS!

AND THE JOURNEY CONTINUES....

About the Author

Celena Powell is the Founder and CEO of F.L. Y. Woman 2 Woman Talk, Ministries, a meetup group that was established in 2016. This meetup currently serves more than 350 Women in the greater Cleveland Ohio area. The Vision of F.L.Y. Woman 2 Woman Talk Ministries is to create a safe environment for women to gather and bond, network be made whole spiritually, mentally, emotionally, financially, and socially.

In 2021 Celena founded and launched the Non-profit "No More Chalk Lines, Inc". This organization is dedicated to Minority Youth and Adult Violence prevention. Losing her nephew in August of 2020 to gun violence, reignited her passion for "grassroots" community involvement, desiring to save the lives of our young people through hands on, boots on-the-ground engagement."

As an ordained Minister since 2009, Celena has been active in Ministry serving at various capacities, using not only her Spiritual Gifts but also assisting in various administrative support roles in the church as well as Fortune 500 Companies and Non- profit Organizations in the greater Atlanta area.

Since receiving her degree in 2011 in International Global Community Economic
Development from Beulah Heights University, Celena has been on a mission to serve the greater community by volunteering with outreach programs and various other organizations. Having raised two sons as a single parent, Celena endured many hardships and obstacles giving her a heart and passion for Singles and the challenges they face. Her first published book "What the Wrong Kind of Love Taught Me; A Singles Journey to Wholeness, is a six-week study journal requiring the reader to take a hard-inward self-assessment while providing tactics Celena has used to make conscious healthy choices while walking in Singleness.

Celena desires to "Break Singles Out of The Struggle of Singleness"

Contact the Author

www.celenapowell.com

http://www.facebook.com.I-AM-CelenaMarie-102482514737665

http://www.instagram.com/iamcelenamarie/

CELENA1070@GMAIL.COM